A book, too, can be a star, "explosive material, capable of stirring up fresh life endlessly," a living fire to lighten the darkness, leading out into the expanding universe.

—Madeleine L'Engle

T0032822

For Laurie Lane, who lit this fire —C.J.V.

For Maureen Palacios—
and booksellers everywhere who connect
readers to books and to each other —J.A.

Do the best you can, be kind to yourself,
and believe in your dreams —A.L.

Farrar Straus Giroux Books for Young Readers
An imprint of Macmillan Publishing Group, LLC
120 Broadway, New York, NY 10271
mackids.com

Our books may be purchased in bulk for promotional, educational, or
business use. Please contact your local bookseller or the Macmillan Corporate and Premium
Sales Department at (800) 221-7945 ext. 5442 or
by email at MacmillanSpecialMarkets@macmillan.com.

Library of Congress Cataloging-in-Publication Data is available.

First edition, 2022
Color separations by Embassy Graphics
Printed in China by RR Donnelley Asia Printing Solutions Ltd., Dongguan City, Guangdong Province

ISBN 978-0-374-38848-5 (hardcover)
10 9 8 7 6 5 4 3 2 1

The art for this book was created digitally using Procreate, with some elements painted traditionally with gouache.
The text was set in LaGlocondaTT, and the display type was handwritten by the artist. Designed by Marissa Asuncion,
with art direction by Aram Kim. Production was supervised by Susan Doran, and the production editor was Allyson Floridia.
Edited by Grace Kendall, with support from Asia Harden.

A Book, too, can be a Star

The Story of Madeleine L'Engle and
the Making of A Wrinkle in Time

Words by
Charlotte Jones Voiklis & Jennifer Adams

Pictures by
Adelina Lirius

Farrar Straus Giroux ✳ New York

Once, when Madeleine was very small, her parents woke her and took her outside to see the splendor of the starry night sky. It was both dazzlingly dark and full of light, and it seemed to go on forever. She could hear the stars singing, telling her that she was part of something beautiful, generous, and loving.

The singing of the stars filled Madeleine with wonder and excitement, and she realized there was more to her world than daytime and ordinary things. She had big questions.

Madeleine's father was a writer. She liked to watch him work and hear his typewriter *click, click, click*. She saw that he worked very hard. Madeleine understood that writing is a way to ask big questions and look for answers. When she was ten, Madeleine's father gave her his old typewriter. It became one of her most prized possessions.

Madeleine's mother was a pianist. She worked very hard, too,
and Madeleine noticed that if her mother was troubled by something,
playing the piano helped. Music, like writing, is another way to tell
a story, to ask questions, to answer the call of the stars.

Madeleine was an only child and lived with her parents in New York City. In the evenings, her mother and father attended fancy parties with their artist friends, or sometimes went to the opera or symphony. She was often alone, but she was not lonely. Her books kept her company. She found that books answered big questions, sometimes by asking even bigger questions. Even though stars were hard to see in the city, books helped her feel part of a loving and exciting universe.

WHAT ARE MY GIFTS?

WHAT SHOULD I BE WHEN I GROW UP?

WHAT MAKES PEOPLE SAD?

HOW CAN I BE HAPPY?

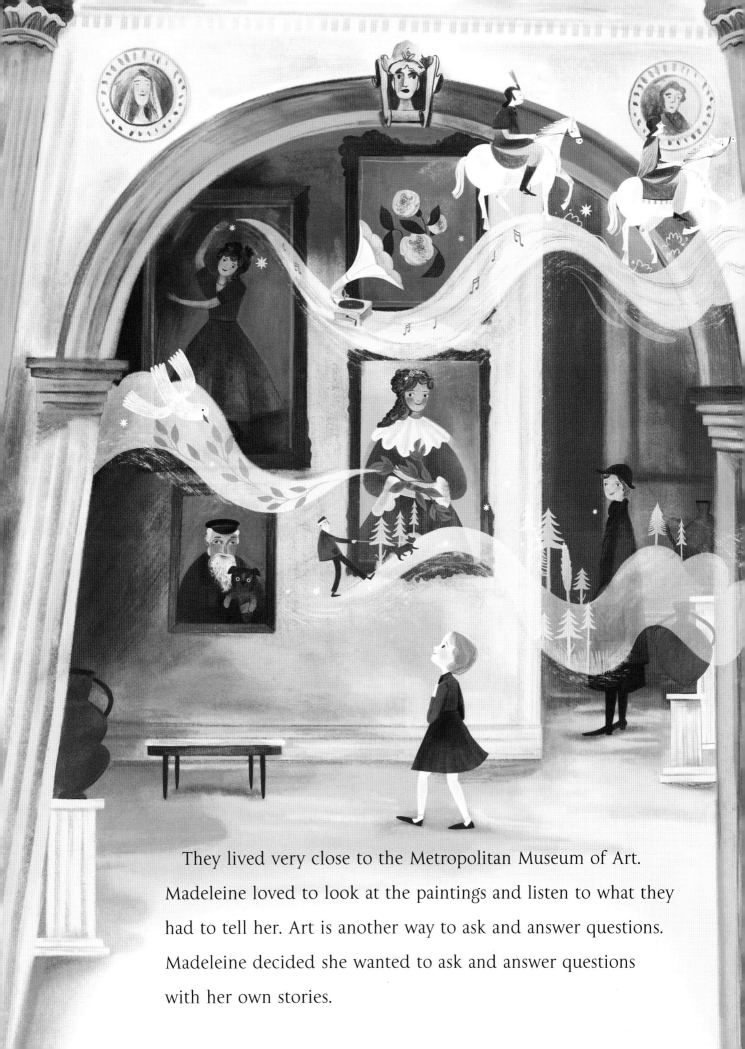

They lived very close to the Metropolitan Museum of Art.
Madeleine loved to look at the paintings and listen to what they
had to tell her. Art is another way to ask and answer questions.
Madeleine decided she wanted to ask and answer questions
with her own stories.

So Madeleine began to write. She wrote stories about famous heroes she knew from books, and stories about little girls like herself. She found that when she had a difficult question, or felt scared or sad or confused, writing could help her feel brave. She learned that a book can be like a star—a new and fiery creation that can shine light into a dark universe.

School was challenging for Madeleine. She was shy and quiet and had a hard time making friends. Her classmates and even her teachers were unkind to her. She changed schools often and was eventually sent to a boarding school. It was very strict, with something to do every moment and little time for daydreaming. The girls were referred to by numbers rather than their names. It was so cold the ink froze in the inkwells.

Now she was never alone, but she *was* lonely. She missed the time she had spent quietly in her room with her books. Sometimes she would try to count the stars through her tiny window at night, to remember what it felt like to be connected to the universe.

She planted poppies in a small garden plot and put the flowers under her pillow, because she had heard that poppies give you wonderful dreams. She fell asleep to visions of grand cities she had never heard of and houses with thousands of rooms for her to explore.

Madeleine continued to write, and using her imagination helped her understand herself and those around her better.

When she changed schools again, she discovered she had become less shy and more able to make friends. She was confident in her stories and began to write and perform in plays.

After college, Madeleine moved back to New York City and lived with other artists in Greenwich Village. It was wartime, and Madeleine, like most people, was often scared and sad. Whenever she felt overwhelmed, she would ride the subway to the planetarium. The stars renewed her sense of wonder and reminded her that even if the world is sometimes a scary place, there are stories to tell and questions to ask.

Madeleine got a job in theater, helping tell stories every night to an audience. Acting is another way of asking questions and looking for

answers. One of her responsibilities was to take care of Touché, a silver poodle in the play. Touché was quite an actor—she would pretend to be a fur stole around Madeleine's neck so she could ride the subway to the theater.

Just as the war was ending, Madeleine published her first novel, *The Small Rain*, about a lonely girl who grows up to be an artist.

While she was working in theater, Madeleine met an actor named Hugh Franklin. At first, she thought they would only be friends, but they fell in love.

MENU

Spaghetti with meatballs, salad, and dessert. 75¢ with wine. 50¢

They listened to each other's stories and knew that a life together would be full of questions and answers and even more questions. It was exciting!

After Madeleine and Hugh were married, they moved to a farmhouse in Connecticut. Hugh ran the general store and Madeleine continued to write. They had three children, many cats, and several dogs.

But publishers kept rejecting Madeleine's new work.
It made her question herself.

WHAT IF MY WRITING ISN'T GOOD?

CAN I REALLY CALL MYSELF A WRITER?

AM I SUCCESSFUL ENOUGH?

SHOULD I KEEP DOING THIS?

Still, Madeleine knew she couldn't give up, even if she wanted to.

When she felt frustrated, she would drive to the top of a nearby mountain.

There, she would watch and listen to the stars. Sometimes the stars

asked more questions than they answered. And that was all right.

When Hugh decided that he also had stories to tell and that he needed to be an actor again, the family moved back to New York City. But first, they took a camping trip all the way across the country.

In a place called the Painted Desert, with its strange shapes and colors and its big skies scattered with stars, Madeleine had an idea for a new kind of book. It was inspired by sonnets and science and her sense of belonging when she looked at the night sky and listened to the stars sing. She began to write, and by the time the family arrived in New York City, she had finished this new book.

At first, publishers rejected it. They said it would be too hard for children to understand and that no grown-up wanted to read a book where children are the heroes.

But they were wrong.

Children and grown-ups loved the book, *A Wrinkle in Time*. It made people ask big questions. And asking questions is very important, even if we don't always find an answer.

Madeleine kept writing, never forgetting what it felt like to look at the stars for the first time or how hard it can be to be a small child in a big universe.

She loved receiving the letters young readers wrote to her. She always responded, encouraging children to write, paint, act, sing, and tell their own stories. She urged them to ask big questions and remember that the world is full of wonder and they belong to it.

After all, the universe is full of questions. And there are
as many different stories as there are stars.

Don't you think?

ONCE UPON A TIME, OR HOW THIS BOOK CAME TO BE

Charlotte knew that she needed to write a picture book biography about her grandmother Madeleine L'Engle as long ago as 2015, when a friend suggested it. And she knew how the book should begin—with the stars. So much of who Madeleine was and what she did began with a glorious star-filled sky, the rhythm of ocean waves, and the taste of salt on the breeze.

Charlotte never considered herself a writer. To her, a writer was someone like her grandmother, someone who only felt alive if she had spent time alone with her paper and pen and the characters and thoughts in her head that day. So at first, Charlotte looked for someone else to write the book. But she soon realized that she had ideas of her own for what she wanted the book to be, and so

she wrote a first draft. Her editor and agent were supportive, but they wanted a different book: a biography of Madeleine for middle-grade readers. Charlotte put her picture book aside and began to work with her sister, Léna Roy, to create *Becoming Madeleine*. The book was published in 2018, and Charlotte and Léna went on a signing tour to promote it. One stop on the tour was at a wonderful independent children's bookstore in Glendale, California, called Once Upon A Time. The store had signed copies of the BabyLit series, which Charlotte admired for their elegance and simplicity, and she was struck by the thought that perhaps Jennifer Adams, the series author, would be the perfect writer to help her with the picture book. She told the owner, Maureen Palacios, of her idea.

Jennifer had been working on BabyLit, retellings of classic novels for the youngest readers, for almost ten years. She was looking for new children's projects to stretch her imagination and challenge her creative writing. One day, on a visit to Glendale, California, she also stopped at the lovely little bookstore called Once Upon A Time.

Jennifer was talking with the store owner and admiring the signed copies of a new book called *Becoming Madeleine*. Maureen noticed her looking at the book and said, "That reminds me—I have something important to tell you." Just then the beloved bookstore cat, Pippi, made a mad dash outside onto the busy street! Maureen ran after her. Once Pippi was safely back inside, Maureen told Jennifer that Charlotte had mentioned wanting to work with her. As soon as she got home, Jennifer had a long phone call with Charlotte. When she hung up from that call, she knew that she and Charlotte were going to become good writing partners and good friends.

Over the next two years, Jennifer and Charlotte worked together back and forth over email, phone, and Google Docs. Sometimes they met for lunch in New York City. Charlotte and Jennifer asked each other lots of questions, wrote and rewrote, and shaped the story of Madeleine that they wanted to tell. Slowly the manuscript for *A Book, Too, Can Be a Star* began to emerge. They were thrilled when Grace Kendall at Farrar Straus Giroux Books for Young Readers wanted to publish the book, and thrilled again when Adelina Lirius agreed to be the illustrator.

Beginnings and Endings

The choice of where to begin the story of this book was clear—with the stars and Madeleine's early vision of them. But the choice of where to end the story was less clear. Many books tell stories of hard work and persistence that pay off in the end, often with fame or material success.

For Madeleine, this was also the case. She didn't give up, and eventually she won the Newbery Medal for *A Wrinkle in Time*, a book that made people see children's literature in a whole new way. Charlotte and Jennifer think it's important to have examples of persistence and courage like this one, of doing things even when they are hard.

They also think, though, that material gain and recognition aren't always the reward, and that the world would be a better place if we learned to broaden our definitions of success. Not everyone will win an award, but every one of us can live a meaningful and fulfilled life by paying attention to the world and people around us and participating in the making and remaking of our communities.

Although this book ends with the unexpected success of *A Wrinkle in Time*, it's not the ending of Madeleine's story. She continued to experiment and take risks with her writing for many more years. We hope *A Book, Too, Can Be a Star* leaves readers with the feeling that questions are more important than answers, that there are many ways to live a creative life, and that every one of us belongs.

MADELEINE'S INFLUENCE

Madeleine and her work have influenced many thousands of people over the years—readers and moviegoers, writers and artists, spiritual seekers, and, most important, children.

To Charlotte, Madeleine taught the value of living a creative life. She showed her that doing the work you love is the most important pursuit—not necessarily how you are recognized with money or praise for that work—and that loving one's family and friends is how we have the biggest impact. Madeleine also influenced Charlotte's work in publishing and preservation in a very real way, since Charlotte is the executor of her grandmother's literary estate.

For Jennifer, Madeleine L'Engle, along with writers like Lloyd Alexander, C. S. Lewis, and George MacDonald, revealed the important influence stories and their tellers can have on young people. In fact, it was the novels she read in grade school that made Jennifer want to write for children when she grew up.

WHY STARS?

My first remembered icon was a heavenly one indeed. It is so important to me that though I have written about it before, I cannot leave it out here. I was a very small child visiting my grandmother at her beach cottage in north Florida. One night someone came into my little room, untucked the mosquito netting from around my crib, and carried me out onto the beach to see the stars. It must have been an unusually beautiful night for someone to have said, "Let's wake up the baby and show her the stars." All I remember is glory.

There were no nearby city lights on the horizon to dim the magnificence of the night.
—MADELEINE L'ENGLE

You already know about Madeleine's early memory of the magnificent night sky and how it influenced the writer throughout her life. More specifically, she loved that human beings are made from the same materials as stars (it's true!) and that the word *disaster* is made up of the Latin root *dis*, meaning "separate," and *aster*, meaning "star," so that *disaster* is literally "separation from the stars."

The stars and the Milky Way are increasingly dim in all parts of the world because of light pollution, or the excessive use of artificial light, such as streetlights and commercial buildings. It's rare that a child today is able to experience the night sky like Madeleine did. Light pollution also has serious consequences for wildlife and ecosystems (artificial light disrupts migration and other patterns), energy consumption (artificial light costs money and other resources), and even our health (artificial light interrupts our sleep cycle).

We wanted to bring your attention to

"Creativity is a way of living life, no matter what our vocation, or how we earn our living."
—Walking on Water

light pollution because the night sky was an important part of how Madeleine nurtured a sense of connection to other beings and to the universe. There are people and organizations all over the world working to reclaim and protect the night sky and educate people about the effects of light pollution and how to take action to prevent it. The International Dark-Sky Association (darksky.org) is a wonderful place to start if you are interested in learning more.

About the Title

The title of this picture book comes from Madeleine's Newbery Medal acceptance speech, "The Expanding Universe." In it she talks about children's books and their ability to help us grow, change, and expand. She quotes an article by Bertha Mahony Miller, a bookstore owner and *The Horn Book* founder, who said that "the bookstore's stock trade is . . . explosive material, capable of stirring up fresh life endlessly." Madeleine builds on Ms. Miller's formulation and says: "A book, too, can be a star, 'explosive material, capable of stirring up fresh life endlessly,' a living fire to lighten the darkness, leading out into the expanding universe."

You can listen to Madeleine L'Engle giving her Newbery Medal acceptance speech on the American Library Association's website.

Further Reading

You can read more about Madeleine's life in *Becoming Madeleine* by Charlotte Jones Voiklis and Léna Roy as well as on her website, MadeleineLEngle.com.

Adult readers may also be interested in *Listening for Madeleine* by Leonard S. Marcus and *A Light So Lovely* by Sarah Arthur.

Madeleine L'Engle's Books for Young Readers

The Time Quintet
A Wrinkle in Time
A Wind in the Door
A Swiftly Tilting Planet
Many Waters
An Acceptable Time

The Austin Family Chronicles
The Twenty-Four Days Before Christmas
Meet the Austins
The Moon by Night
The Young Unicorns
A Ring of Endless Light
Troubling a Star

The O'Keefe Family Chronicles
The Arm of the Starfish
Dragons in the Waters
A House Like a Lotus

Other Works
And Both Were Young
Camilla
The Joys of Love
The Other Dog
Intergalactic P.S. 3

TIME LINE

1918   Madeleine is born on November 29 in New York City to Madeleine Hall Barnett and Charles Wadsworth Camp. Her father was a soldier in the US Army during World War I, and did not return home until the following spring.

1929   Madeleine wins the poetry prize at school. The Great Depression begins.

1930   The family moves to Europe, and Madeleine is enrolled at a girls' boarding school in Switzerland.

1933   They return to the United States. Madeleine attends another girls' boarding school in Charleston, South Carolina.

1936   Madeleine's father falls gravely ill from pneumonia and dies.

1941   Madeleine graduates cum laude from Smith College and moves to New York City with her best friend. America enters World War II.

1942   Madeleine auditions for Margaret Webster and Eva Le Gallienne and gets her debut Broadway role, a small part in *The Cherry Orchard*.

1943   Madeleine begins using her middle name, L'Engle, on the stories and plays she sends out.

1944   Madeleine sells her first novel, *The Small Rain*. She meets Hugh Franklin, who joins the touring company of *The Cherry Orchard*.

1945   *The Small Rain* is published to strong sales and a positive reception by critics.

1946   Hugh and Madeleine marry. They buy an old farmhouse in Goshen, Connecticut, as a weekend home and begin a family.

1947   Madeleine's second novel, *Ilsa*, is published. Her mother is unhappy with it because she thinks it embarrasses the family.

1947   Daughter Josephine is born.